Earaches

By Sharon Gordon

Consultant
Nanci R. Vargus, Ed.D.
Assistant Professor
Literacy Education
University of Indianapolis
Indianapolis, Indiana

Jayne L. Waddell, R.N., M.A., L.P.C.
School Nurse/Health Educator/Lic. Professional Counselor

Children's Press®
A Division of Scholastic Inc.
New York   Toronto   London   Auckland   Sydney
Mexico City   New Delhi   Hong Kong
Danbury, Connecticut

Designer: Herman Adler Design
Photo Researcher: Caroline Anderson
The photo on the cover shows a doctor checking a boy's ear.

Library of Congress Cataloging-in-Publication Data

Gordon, Sharon.
  Earaches / by Sharon Gordon.
    p. cm. — (Rookie read-about health)
Includes index.
Summary: Simple text explains what earaches are, what causes them, and
common ways to prevent them.
  ISBN 0-516-22584-7 (lib. bdg.)   0-516-27397-3 (pbk.)
  1. Earache in children—Juvenile literature. [1. Earache. 2. Medical
care.] I. Title. II. Series.
  RF291.5.C45 G67 2003
  618.92'0978—dc21
                                        2002015124

CHILDREN'S PRESS, AND ROOKIE READ-ABOUT®,
and associated logos are trademarks and or registered trademarks
of Grolier Publishing Co., Inc. SCHOLASTIC and associated logos
are trademarks and or registered trademarks of Scholastic Inc.

1 2 3 4 5 6 7 8 9 10 R 12 11 10 09 08 07 06 05 04 03

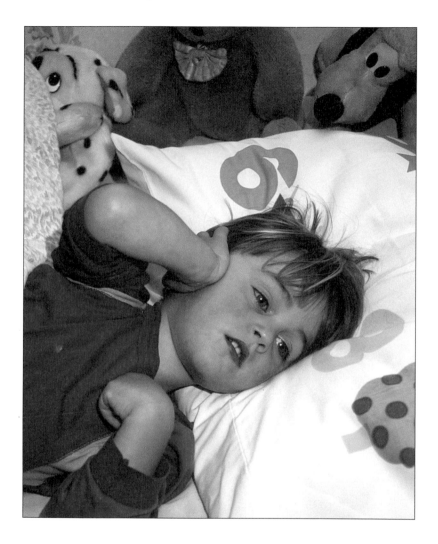

My ear hurts!

What is wrong with it?

You might have an earache.

An earache is a pain in the ear. It can start very quickly.

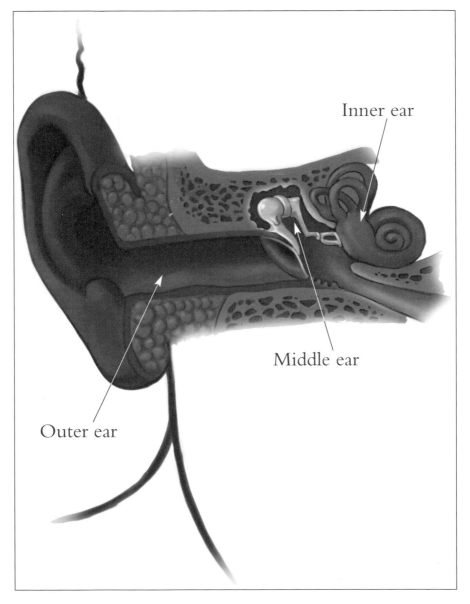

Inner ear

Middle ear

Outer ear

The pain you feel is from the middle ear.

The middle ear is inside your head.

The Eustachian (you-STAY-she-in) tube goes from your middle ear to your nose and throat.

The tube lets air go back and forth. It is supposed to be open.

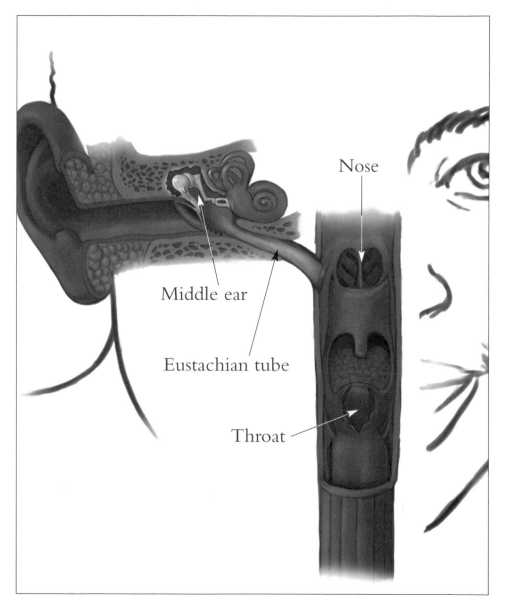

Nose

Middle ear

Eustachian tube

Throat

When you have a cold,
the tube can get blocked.

Air cannot get through.
Germs start to grow.

You have an *infection*.

Your body tries to fight the germs.

It sends in special cells called white blood cells.

Pus begins to form. The pus makes your ear hurt.

Germ

White blood cells

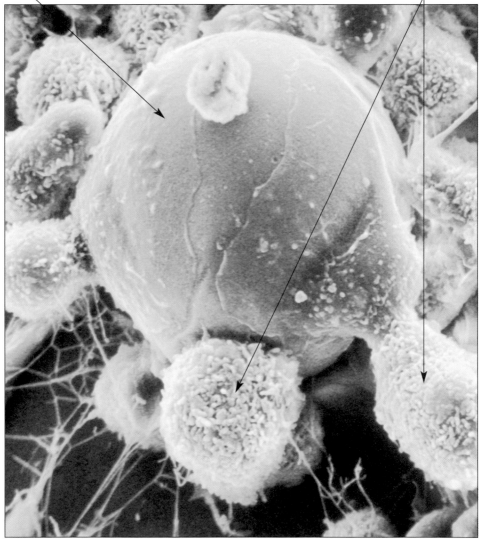

White blood cells attacking a germ

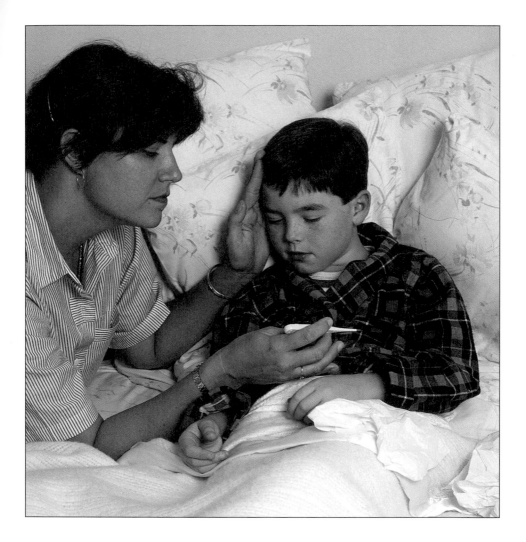

You might have a fever, too.

Sometimes, you get an earache in both ears!
It becomes hard to hear.

Tell your parents whenever your ear hurts.

You may need to see the doctor.

The doctor has a tiny
flashlight. It helps him
see deep into your ear.
He can see if it is red
and swollen.

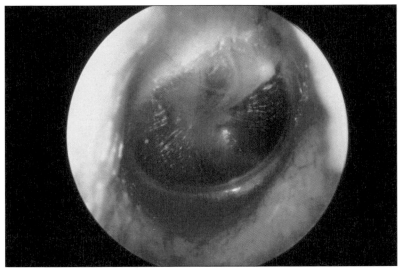

How a healthy ear looks inside

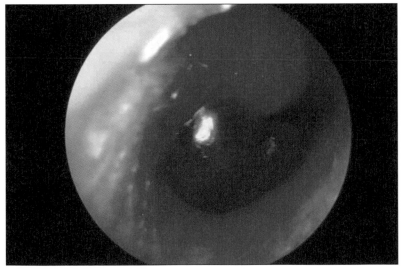

How an infected ear looks inside

You may need to take an
antibiotic (ANT-i-by-OT-ic).
The antibiotic will cure
the infection.

The medicine works quickly. In a day or two, you will start to feel much better.

Children have more earaches than adults do. The tubes in children's ears are short.

As you grow, so do the tubes. It is harder for them to become blocked.

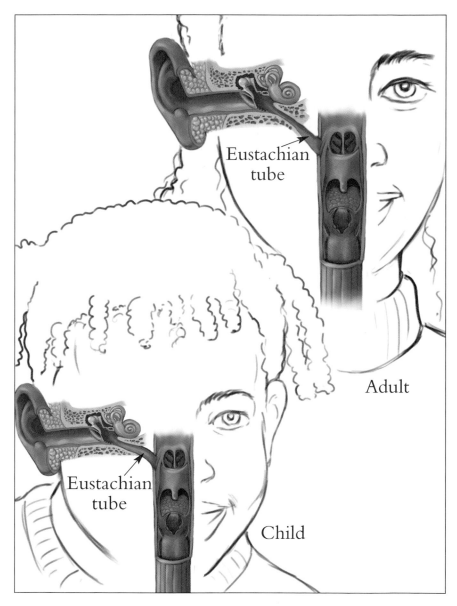

Eustachian
tube

Adult

Eustachian
tube

Child

24

You cannot catch an earache from someone else, but you can catch a cold from someone.

A cold might lead to an earache.

So try to stay healthy.

Do not get too close to people who have colds.

Wash your hands often. Keep them away from your face.

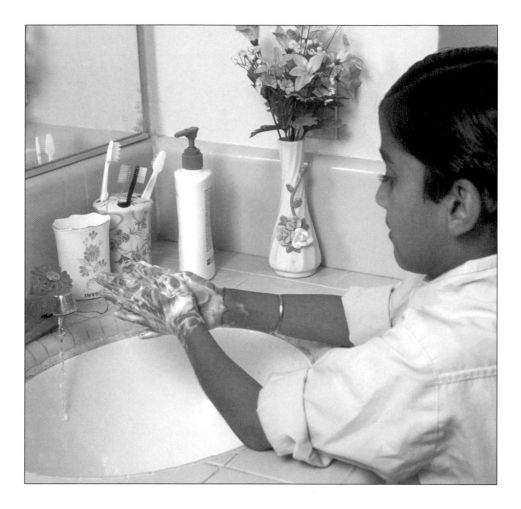

Do you hear?

Words You Know

antibiotic

earache

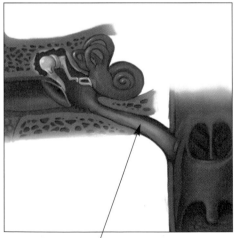

Eustachian tube

fever

30

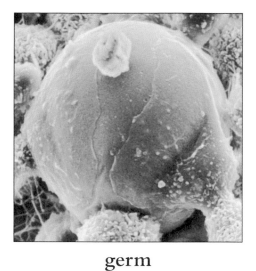

germ

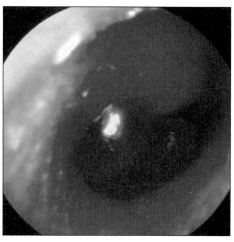

infection

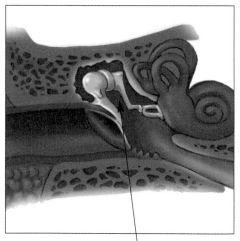

middle ear

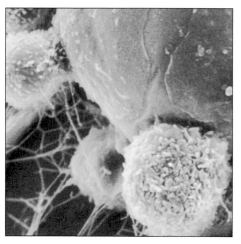

white blood cells

Index

About the Author

Sharon Gordon is a writer living in Midland Park, New Jersey. She and her husband have three school-aged children and a spoiled pooch. Together they enjoy visiting the Outer Banks of North Carolina as often as possible.

Photo Credits

Photographs © 2003: Corbis Images/Todd Gipstein: 15; Custom Medical Stock Photo/NMSB: 19 bottom, 19 top; Dembinsky Photo Assoc./Patti McConville: 14; Peter Arnold Inc./Manfred Kage: 13; Photo Researchers, NY: 3 (Mark Clarke), 18 (Blair Seitz); PhotoEdit: 10, 20, 27 (Mary Kate Denny), 21 (Myrleen Ferguson), cover (Michael Newman), 24 (David Young-Wolff); The Image Works/Ellen Senisi: 16; Visuals Unlimited: 5 (Eric Anderson), 28 (Jeff Greenberg).